FUN FACT FILE: FOUNDING FATHERS

20 FUN FACTS ABOUT GEORGE WASHINGTON

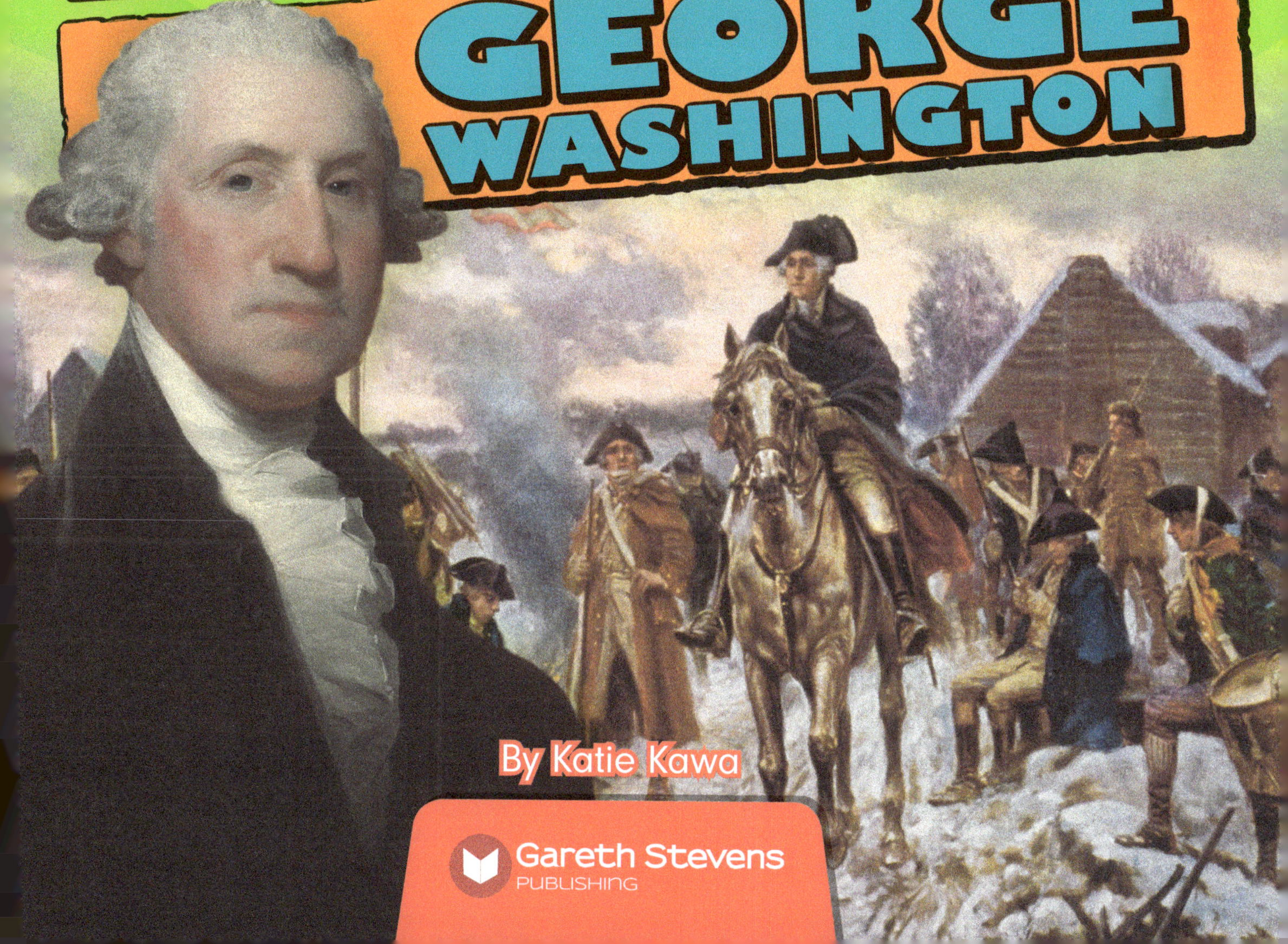

By Katie Kawa

Gareth Stevens
PUBLISHING

Please visit our website, www.garethstevens.com. For a free color catalog of all our high-quality books, call toll free 1-800-542-2595 or fax 1-877-542-2596.

Library of Congress Cataloging-in-Publication Data

Names: Kawa, Katie, author.
Title: 20 fun facts about George Washington / Katie Kawa.
Other titles: Twenty fun facts about George Washington
Description: New York : Gareth Stevens Publishing, [2018] | Series: Fun fact file: the founding fathers | Includes index.
Identifiers: LCCN 2017000904| ISBN 9781538202906 (pbk. book) | ISBN 9781538202722 (6 pack) | ISBN 9781538202845 (library bound book)
Subjects: LCSH: Washington, George, 1732-1799–Juvenile literature. | Presidents–United States–Biography–Juvenile literature. | Generals–United States–Biography–Juvenile literature.
Classification: LCC E312.66 .K425 2018 | DDC 973.4/1092 [B] –dc23
LC record available at https://lccn.loc.gov/2017000904

First Edition

Published in 2018 by
Gareth Stevens Publishing
111 East 14th Street, Suite 349
New York, NY 10003

Designer: Sam DeMartin
Editor: Ryan Nagelhout

Photo credits: Cover, p. 1 (portrait) Everett - Art/Shutterstock.com; cover, pp. 1 (background), 5 Education Images/UIG/Getty Images; p. 8 Kean Collection/Archive Photos/Getty Images; p. 9 Jorge Salcedo/Shutterstock.com; p. 10 Sipley/ClassicStock/Getty Images; p. 11 Hulton Archive/Hulton Archive/Getty Images; p. 12 Ipsumpix/Corbis Historical/Getty Images; pp. 13, 19 Interim Archives/Archive Photos/Getty Images; pp. 14, 17, 22 Everett Historical/Shutterstock.com; p. 15 karen roach/Shutterstock.com; p. 16 PhotosByAndy/Shutterstock.com; p. 18 Themadchopper/Wikimedia Commons; p. 21 Bardocz Peter/Shutterstock.com; p. 23 Steve Heap/Shutterstock.com; p. 24 PhotoQuest/Archive Photos/Getty Images; p. 25 Stock Montage/Archive Photos/Getty Images; p. 26 MPI/Archive Photos/Getty Images; p. 27 Jeremy R. Smith Sr./Shutterstock.com; p. 29 mandritoiu/Shutterstock.com.

Printed in the United States of America

CPSIA compliance information: Batch #CS17GS: For further information contact Gareth Stevens, New York, New York at 1-800-542-2595.

Contents

Words in the glossary appear in **bold** type the first time they are used in the text.

A Famous Founding Father

What do you know about George Washington? You probably know he was the first president of the United States. You might also know he led American soldiers as they fought for freedom from the British in the American Revolution. Maybe you even know he lived in a big house in Virginia called Mount Vernon.

There's so much more to learn, though—from the names of his dogs to the truth about his teeth. Read on to find out fun facts about this Founding Father!

George Washington is sometimes called the "Father of His Country."

No School for George!

FACT 1

George Washington stopped going to school when he was 15.

Not a lot is known for sure about Washington's childhood, but it is known his **formal** education ended when he was around 15 years old. He didn't even go to **college**!

His father, Augustine, died when George was 11 years old, and there wasn't enough money to send George away to college. Instead, he trained as a **surveyor** and read math books to get better at this job.

Because Washington is so famous, many myths, or larger-than-life stories, have been created about him over time. Now you know the truth behind the myths!

George Washington: Myth and Truth

MYTH

George Washington was given an ax as a gift when he was a child, and he used it to chop at his father's cherry tree. When his father asked him what happened to the tree, George said he couldn't tell a lie; he cut the tree.

FACT

This story, which was meant to show young George's honesty, most likely never happened. It was invented by a writer named Mason Locke Weems.

MYTH

George Washington once threw a silver dollar across the Potomac River.

FACT

It was reported by Washington's great-grandson that he once threw a piece of slate across the Rappahannock River, which is much narrower than the Potomac.

MYTH

George Washington had wooden teeth.

FACT

He did have fake teeth, but they were made of things such as ivory, human and animal teeth, gold, and lead—not wood.

MYTH

George Washington wore a wig.

FACT

It might look like Washington's white hair was a wig, but it was actually his real hair that was powdered.

FACT 2

Washington helped start a world war.

In May 1754, Washington led British troops to fight the French in the Ohio River valley in southwestern Pennsylvania. This fighting sparked what became known as the Seven Years' War around the world and the French and Indian War in North America.

Washington fought for the British as part of the Virginia **militia** during the French and Indian War.

FACT 3

Two of Washington's horses were shot in the same battle!

During the Battle of the Monongahela in July 1755, Washington lost two horses when they were shot while he was sitting on them. In the same battle, Washington's coat was hit with four **musket** balls, but he wasn't hurt!

Washington was a great horseback rider. His horses, though, were not always so lucky!

FACT 4

Washington lost more battles than he won.

Washington is thought of as a great military leader because he helped America win its independence from Britain. He led his troops and kept their spirits up in hard times. But they were not always successful—Washington lost battles at White Plains, Fort Necessity, and other places, too!

Washington served as commander of the Continental army during the American Revolution, which lasted from 1775 to 1783.

FACT 5

No one will ever rank higher than Washington in the US military.

In 1976, President Jimmy Carter appointed Washington General of the Armies. This is the highest military rank anyone in the United States can have. Washington is actually considered a six-star general!

Washington's military leadership made him the popular choice to lead the United States as its first president.

Leading the Revolution

FACT 6

George Washington once started a riot!

Washington read the Declaration of Independence to his troops and to citizens in New York City on July 9, 1776. Later, the crowds who heard him read it tore down a monument of King George III of Britain.

The Declaration of Independence was officially adopted on July 4, 1776. Washington read it to his troops 5 days later.

FACT 7

Washington was popular, but not everyone liked him.

During the American Revolution, certain military leaders, including Major General Charles Lee, didn't like the way Washington was running the army. Lieutenant Colonel John Laurens even challenged Lee to a **duel** because Lee had been speaking poorly about Washington's character.

The First President

FACT 8

Everyone voted for Washington!

In 1789, George Washington was elected the first president of the United States by a group known as the Electoral College. Every member of the Electoral College voted for him. Washington is the only president so far to have the support of the entire Electoral College.

Every member of the Electoral College voted for Washington again in 1792.

FACT 9

Washington didn't like parties—at least not political ones.

Washington is the only president to be elected without being part of any political party. When he left the presidency, he warned against political parties. In his 1796 Farewell Address, he said they could **divide** and hurt the country.

Today's political parties are different from the ones that came about after Washington was president.

FACT 10

Washington was a very rich president.

It's believed that Washington's personal fortune was as much as $525 million in today's money. He owned a large amount of land, including Mount Vernon. That's where most of his wealth came from.

Mount Vernon, which is the name of Washington's Virginia home, was a very large farm, which is also known as a plantation.

FACT 11

Washington had to borrow money to start his new job!

Washington's land made him rich, but he didn't have a lot of actual money. In fact, he had to borrow money to move to New York City to start his first term as president!

When Washington was first elected president, New York City was the capital of the United States.

Stepping Up and Stepping Down

FACT 12

Washington was a hands-on commander in chief!

In the early 1790s, farmers in western Pennsylvania pushed back against new taxes suggested by the national government. Washington led troops into Pennsylvania in 1794 to fight these farmers during what was known as the Whiskey Rebellion.

The presence of Washington and his troops helped put an end to the Whiskey Rebellion.

FACT 13

Washington didn't want to be president forever.

Unlike presidents today, Washington didn't have to leave office after two terms. Instead, he chose to step down and live among the American people at Mount Vernon.

By stepping down after two terms, Washington set a precedent, or example for other presidents. Only Franklin D. Roosevelt served more than two terms.

FACT 14

Washington wasn't a world traveler.

In 1751, Washington traveled to the Caribbean island of Barbados with his half-brother Lawrence. This was the only time in his life he traveled outside what's now the United States. Even as president, he didn't visit any other countries.

While in Barbados, Washington came down with smallpox. This sickness took the lives of millions of people, but Washington survived. He then became immune to the disease, which means he couldn't get it again.

Important Places in WASHINGTON'S LIFE

Washington didn't travel too far from home during his lifetime.

Life at Mount Vernon

FACT 15

The Washingtons didn't have any children of their own.

George didn't have any children with his wife Martha. However, there were plenty of kids around Mount Vernon. The Washingtons raised Martha's two children from her first marriage, and they helped care for nieces, nephews, and grandchildren.

Martha Washington

Martha and George had a strong marriage. She spent almost half of the American Revolution by her husband's side.

FACT 16

After his death, Washington freed his slaves.

Washington owned slaves. However, he wrote in his **will** that after he and his wife died, all his slaves should be freed. He was one of the only Founding Fathers to free his slaves.

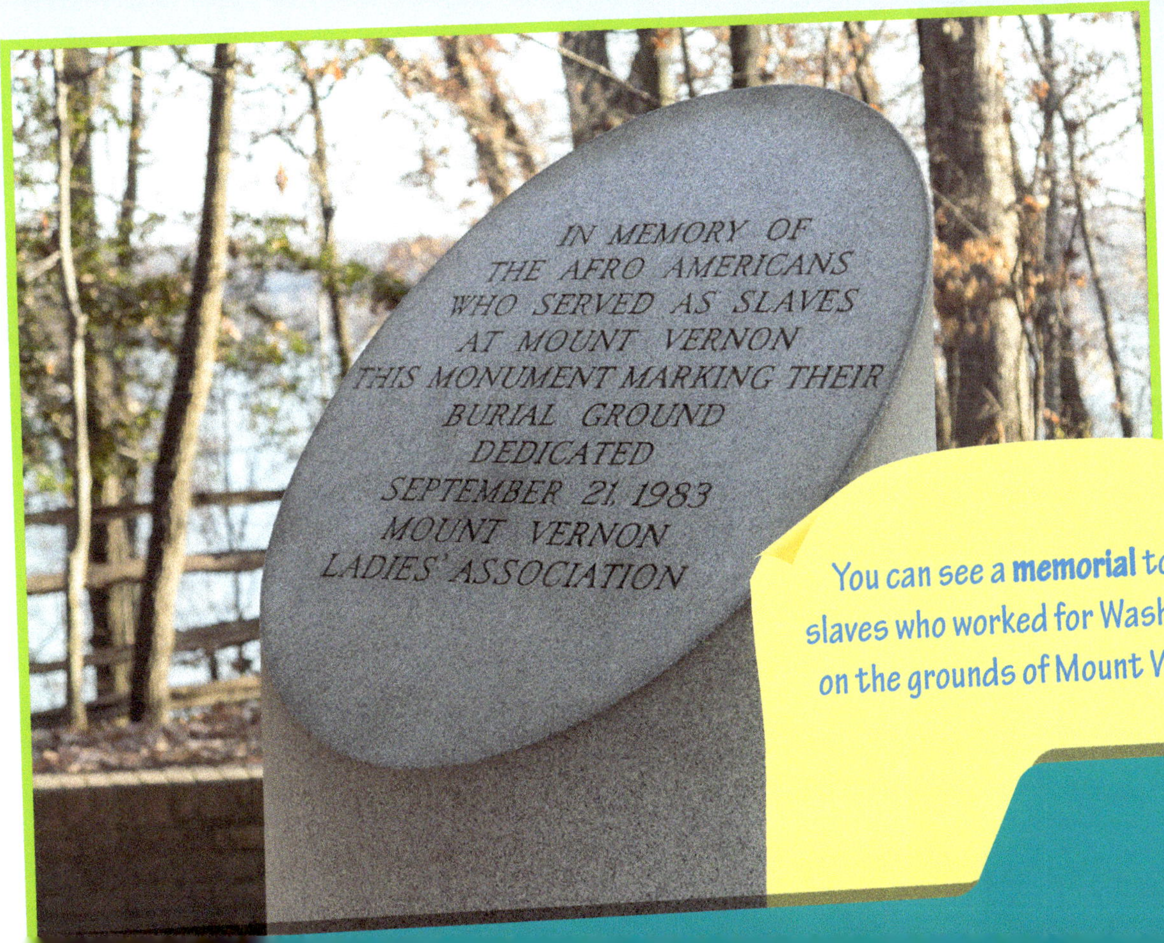

You can see a **memorial** to the slaves who worked for Washington on the grounds of Mount Vernon.

In Washington's time, dances were very formal. You had to know the right steps!

FACT 17

The dance floor was one of Washington's favorite places.

Washington took dance lessons when he was a young man. He loved dancing and became known as a good dancer. Dancing was an important part of parties during Washington's time.

FACT 18

The dogs at Mount Vernon had crazy names!

Washington loved dogs, and his dogs often went hunting with him. They were important members of his family. He gave them names that included Tipsy, Taster, Truelove, and Sweet Lips.

Washington wrote about his dogs in his diaries, which is how we know some of their names.

Back from the Dead?

FACT 19

Washington was afraid of being buried alive.

On December 14, 1799, George Washington died after getting sick with a sore throat. A few hours before he died, he asked not to be buried until 3 days after his death. He was afraid people would think he was dead and bury him before he really died.

Doctors at the time of Washington's death believed letting blood out of the body could help sick people. They took 40 percent of Washington's blood out of his body when he was dying!

FACT 20

Someone tried to bring Washington back from the dead!

After Washington died, Dr. William Thornton believed he could bring him back to life. He thought he could do this by warming up Washington's body, opening a path to his lungs, and giving him blood from a lamb.

Thornton wanted Washington to be buried at the US Capitol, which Washington helped **design**. However, he was buried at Mount Vernon because he wanted to remain at home—and with Martha—forever.

Keeping His Memory Alive

George Washington was honored in many ways after his death. The nation's capital—where all other presidents lived and worked—is named after him. He's also the only president to have a state named after him.

Washington's face is carved into Mount Rushmore alongside other great presidents. You can even visit the Washington Monument in Washington, DC, and tour Mount Vernon if you go to Virginia. These are just some of the ways Washington's memory has been kept alive in the country he helped build.

When the Washington Monument was built in 1884, it was the tallest building in the world!

Glossary

college: a school students attend after high school

design: to make a plan for how to make something

divide: to separate

duel: a fight between two people, often using weapons and having witnesses

formal: done according to rules or forms

memorial: something built to honor or remember a person or event

militia: a group of citizens with some military training who are called to active duty in an emergency

musket: a kind of long gun used in the past

riot: a public disorder during which a group of angry people becomes noisy and out of control

surveyor: a person whose job is to find and report on the size, shape, and borders of a piece of land

will: a legal piece of writing that spells out how someone's property should be dealt with after they die

For More Information

Books

Murray, Robb. *The Washington Monument: Myths, Legends, and Facts.* North Mankato, MN: Capstone Press, 2015.

Olesen, Andrew. *George Washington: America's History Maker.* New York, NY: PowerKids Press, 2016.

Yasuda, Anita. *The New Nation Through the Eyes of George Washington.* Minneapolis, MN: Core Library, 2016.

Websites

George Washington
whitehouse.gov/1600/presidents/georgewashington
The White House's George Washington page features a short biography, as well as links to information about Martha Washington.

George Washington: A Resource Guide
loc.gov/rr/program/bib/presidents/washington/memory.html
The Library of Congress has links to many digital collections of primary sources written by or about George Washington.

George Washington's Mount Vernon
mountvernon.org
The official website of George Washington's home has articles about Washington, lists of fun facts, and information to help you plan your own trip to Mount Vernon.

Publisher's note to educators and parents: Our editors have carefully reviewed these websites to ensure that they are suitable for students. Many websites change frequently, however, and we cannot guarantee that a site's future contents will continue to meet our high standards of quality and educational value. Be advised that students should be closely supervised whenever they access the Internet.

Index